Dominik Piehlmaier

Irrational and Overrated:

Is our Unrealistic Self-Perception connected to Educational Achievements?

Anchor Compact

Piehlmaier, Dominik: Irrational and Overrated: Is our Unrealistic Self-Perception connected to Educational Achievements? Hamburg, Anchor Academic Publishing 2013
Original title of the thesis: Overconfidence - A Matter of Education?

Buch-ISBN: 978-3-95489-075-0
PDF-eBook-ISBN: 978-3-95489-575-5
Druck/Herstellung: Anchor Academic Publishing, Hamburg, 2013Additionally:
Fachhochschule Kufstein Tirol, Tirol, Austria, Bachelor Thesis, 2012

Bibliografische Information der Deutschen Nationalbibliothek:
Die Deutsche Nationalbibliothek verzeichnet diese Publikation in der Deutschen Nationalbibliografie; detaillierte bibliografische Daten sind im Internet über http://dnb.d-nb.de abrufbar

Bibliographical Information of the German National Library:
The German National Library lists this publication in the German National Bibliography. Detailed bibliographic data can be found at: http://dnb.d-nb.de

All rights reserved. This publication may not be reproduced, stored in a retrieval system or transmitted, in any form or by any means, electronic, mechanical, photocopying, recording or otherwise, without the prior permission of the publishers.

Das Werk einschließlich aller seiner Teile ist urheberrechtlich geschützt. Jede Verwertung außerhalb der Grenzen des Urheberrechtsgesetzes ist ohne Zustimmung des Verlages unzulässig und strafbar. Dies gilt insbesondere für Vervielfältigungen, Übersetzungen, Mikroverfilmungen und die Einspeicherung und Bearbeitung in elektronischen Systemen.

Die Wiedergabe von Gebrauchsnamen, Handelsnamen, Warenbezeichnungen usw. in diesem Werk berechtigt auch ohne besondere Kennzeichnung nicht zu der Annahme, dass solche Namen im Sinne der Warenzeichen- und Markenschutz-Gesetzgebung als frei zu betrachten wären und daher von jedermann benutzt werden dürften.

Die Informationen in diesem Werk wurden mit Sorgfalt erarbeitet. Dennoch können Fehler nicht vollständig ausgeschlossen werden und die Diplomica Verlag GmbH, die Autoren oder Übersetzer übernehmen keine juristische Verantwortung oder irgendeine Haftung für evtl. verbliebene fehlerhafte Angaben und deren Folgen.

Alle Rechte vorbehalten

© Anchor Academic Publishing, ein Imprint der Diplomica® Verlag GmbH
http://www.diplom.de, Hamburg 2013
Printed in Germany

For Tabea, my dear little sister.

May you gain confidence and find your way again.

I   ACKNOWLEDGMENT

This study was not simply conducted to obtain an academic degree. It was motivated by the same curiosity that makes children wonder why the earth is moving or why some stars shine brighter than others. I had some unanswered questions and the only way to solve this was to create a questionnaire and conduct field research. However, just like in many other situations in life, I could not have done it on my own. Fortunately, I have met many constructive and wise people on my way who have been willing to help me out.

The names of those who influenced this book the most are unfamiliar to me, yet they deserve special recognition. I would like to thank the hundreds of students, who participated in this study. All of this would not have been possible without their contributions. The individual who supported me the most throughout the empirical research and the writing process is Jennifer Pfister. I thank her for pre-testing the questionnaire and listening to my findings so uncomplainingly. I feel privileged to have had many enthusiastic and kind teachers who did not only share their knowledge with me but also dedicated their precious time to collect data for this book. Among those I am particularly grateful to Edgar Kempter, who is an inspiring pedagogue and a true supporter, to Florian Parzefall, a classicist in German literature, who awakened my interest in writing, to Adrian Pickel, who has the unique ability to spread happiness and confidence to those who listen to him, to Sabine Ruetz, whose articulacy and in-depth knowledge in journalism constantly animated me, and to Stefan Neuhauser for reminding me of the importance of history. Special thanks go to my dear cousin Tobias Henniger, who had the resilience to help me with this research while also taking care of his young family and his students. I am indebted to my good friend Martin Deininger for his erudition and his efforts to gather data from his degree program. I would like to thank Joanie Andelin for proofreading this book even though she had little time and for her kindness to forgive me my mistakes. Finally, I am deeply grateful to Claudia Bauer and Manfred Nacke for their contributions to this study. They knew me so little and helped me so much – this is true magnanimousness.

TABLE OF CONTENTS

I	Acknowledgment	I
II	List of Graphs	III
III	Abbreviations	IV
IV	Abstract	V
1	**Overconfidence: The Harmful Optimism**	1
1.1	Background and Motivation	2
1.2	Definition: Overconfidence	3
1.2.1	Unrealistic Optimism	4
1.2.2	Better-Than-Average Effect	5
1.2.3	Illusion of Control	5
1.2.4	Illusion of Knowledge	6
1.2.5	Self-serving bias	7
1.2.6	Summary	8
1.3	Structure	9
2	**Methodology**	9
3	**The German Education System**	11
3.1	Federal Differences	12
3.2	Influences of the Bologna Process	13
4	**Review of Literature**	15
4.1	Confounders of Overconfidence	17
4.1.1	Gender	17
4.1.2	Age	18
4.1.3	Mental Health	19
4.1.4	Euphoria	19
4.1.5	Education	20

4.2	Criticism	21
5	**Empirical Research**	**23**
5.1	Hypothesis	23
5.2	Process of Primary Data Collection	25
5.3	Findings	26
5.4	Interpretation	28
6	**Conclusion**	**29**
V	**Bibliography**	**32**
VI	**Appendix**	**A**

II LIST OF GRAPHS

Figure 1:	Five Factors of Overconfidence	8
Figure 2:	German Education System	11
Figure 3:	Bavarian Education System	13
Figure 4:	Development of Erasmus Students per Year	14

III Abbreviations

NPP	Nuclear Power Plant
NISA	Japanese Nuclear and Industrial Safety Agency
INES	International Nuclear and Radiological Event Scale
BTAE	Better-Than-Average Effect
IOC	Illusion of Control
SSB	Self-Serving Bias
CI	Confidence Interval
PISA	Program for International Student Assessment
ISCED	International Standard Classification of Education
SSS	Specialized Secondary School
UAS	University of Applied Sciences
QLSGEC	Qualifying Lower Secondary General Education Certificate
GCSE	General Certificate of Secondary Education
GCUE	General Certificate for University Entrance
GCUASE	General Certificate for University of Applied Sciences Entrance
ECTS	European Credit Transfer and Accumulation System
TUM	Technical University Munich
NRW	North Rhine-Westphalia
SE	Standard Error
ANOVA	Analysis of Variance

IV ABSTRACT

FH Kufstein

Degree program: International Business and Management FT-10

Overconfidence – A Matter of Education?

Student: Dominik Piehlmaier

Disclaimer: In the interest of a reader-friendly flow of text, gender-neutral terminology has been used wherever possible. If a non-neutral form appears, it automatically refers to both genders.

This work examines the relationship between education and excessive confidence in situations of uncertainty. For this purpose, a questionnaire with 10 pseudo general knowledge questions was designed, whereby their degree of difficulty exceeds the knowledge of an average student by far. It was investigated whether subjects (N = 535) would acknowledge this condition and its associated nescience. If that is the case, they will answer the 10 questions within an extremely wide confidence interval in order to meet the predefined 90% accuracy requirement. The focus of investigation was in Southern Germany, as the school system regularly receives top marks in national educational rankings. The data analysis resulted in the stochastic proof that there are significant differences between the various educational institutions in accuracy and overconfidence.

In addition to the empirical study the paper defines the distortion of judgment and identifies its relevant factors. It gives a detailed explanation of the German education system and states the criticism of the concept of overconfidence. The paper concludes with a recommendation for action and ventures a look ahead.

Kufstein, July 10, 2012

FH Kufstein

Studiengang: Internationale Wirtschaft und Management VZ-10

Ist Vertrauens-Hypertrophie bildungsabhängig?

Student: Dominik Piehlmaier

Hinweis: Die in dieser Arbeit gewählte männliche Form bezieht sich gleichermaßen auf weibliche Personen. Eine Doppelbezeichnung wurde ausschließlich aufgrund einfacherer Lesbarkeit nicht gewählt.

Diese Arbeit untersucht den Zusammenhang zwischen Bildung und übermäßigem Selbstvertrauen in Situationen von Ungewissheit. Dazu wurde ein Fragebogen mit 10 Quasi-Allgemeinwissensfragen entwickelt, wobei deren Schwierigkeitsgrad das Wissen eines durchschnittlichen Schülers bei Weitem übersteigt. Es wurde untersucht, ob die Probanden (N=535) diesen Zustand und ihre damit verbundene Unwissenheit anerkennen und zur Beantwortung der 10 Fragen, innerhalb eines vorgegebenen 90% Konfidenzintervalls, jenen Vertrauensbereich möglichst weit wählen, um die Anforderungen zu erfüllen. Der Fokus der Untersuchung lag in Süddeutschland, da das dortige Schulsystem regelmäßig Bestnoten im nationalen Bildungsvergleich erhält. Die Datenauswertung resultiert in der Erbringung des stochastischen Beweises, dass es zwischen den Bildungseinrichtungen einen signifikanten Unterschied beim Schätzverhalten und der damit verbundenen Vertrauens-Hypertrophie gibt.

Neben der empirischen Untersuchung definiert die Arbeit den Begriff des übermäßigen Selbstvertrauens und benennt die relevanten Einflussfaktoren. Das deutsche Bildungssystem wird dabei ebenso beleuchtet, wie die Kritik am Konzept der Heuristik. Die Abhandlung endet mit einer Handlungsempfehlung und einem Ausblick in die Zukunft.

Kufstein, 10. Juli 2012

1 OVERCONFIDENCE: THE HARMFUL OPTIMISM

The ability to expect a rosy future and solidly trust in our skills empower us to create monuments of human capability and push mankind toward unexpected technological findings. Marie Curie and her husband Pierre found the fission products radium and polonium and developed the first methods to isolate them in order to use both for further research (Nobel Lectures, 1967). The Chinese Ming Empire finished the Great Wall of China, the biggest man-made structure ever built, in 1620 (UNESCO World Heritage Centre, 2011). Every year millions of people start their own business all around the world; others get married and start a family. Every person who makes such a decision does it because of their faith in their own actions. It is, however, uncertain whether Marie Curie would have continued her intensive research with radium if she had known that radiation causes severe illnesses. It can be seen as certain that the Ming Emperors would not have reconstructed the Great Wall if they had been informed that it would not protect them from being replaced by the Manchurian Qing Dynasty.[1]

This is not only true for historical events, but also for modern decision making. If US Americans decide to get married, most do not take into account that they could be the one out of three couples that divorce (U.S. Census Bureau, 2012). In 1993, when the U.S. divorce rate was close to 50%, a study tested whether people are aware of these numbers before they tied the knot. Although the subjects knew the facts, not one of them thought that this would happen to their relationship (Baker and Emery, 1993). This was unexplainably optimistic and on average not true for almost every second couple. Startup owners tend to share the same view of their business ideas. In a well-known survey, entrepreneurs rated their expected business success. 81% of the 2,994 participating founders thought that their chances of success were 70% or higher. Every third person stated that his chances were not less than 100% (Cooper et al., 1988). These expectations seem unrealistically high compared to research showing a different picture. 34% of all U.S. firms do not get through the first year, and half of the companies go out of business before the end of the second year. 60% do not survive the third year (Wiklund, 2006). A HBS article paints an even worse scenario:

---

[1] In fact the cost of maintenance and defense for the Wall were one reason for the decline of the Ming Dynasty.

30 to 40% of investors lose most or all of their assets; 70 to 80% of all startups do not achieve the expected return on investment and 90 to 95 of them fall short of meeting their declared goal. In other words *"failure is the norm"* (Nobel, 2011).

This might be one of the best examples of the discrepancy between unrealistic optimism and reality. The too rosy estimation of their own abilities and the business environment foils many startup founders. At the same time, some companies survive and contribute to society for exactly the same reasons. In that sense, overconfidence is often but not always harmful. There are other examples of this psychological phenomenon showing its destructive side. Dozens of nuclear power plants (NPPs) were built in earthquake risk areas especially in Japan, India and the State of California. In the aftermath of the 2004 Tsunami which destroyed huge coastal areas in Indonesia, Sri Lanka, India and Thailand, the Japanese Nuclear and Industrial Safety Agency (NISA) launched a study to assess the risk of a tsunami for Japanese NPPs. There was a special interest in those plants which face the Pacific without any protective islands off the coast. Two years later the results suggested that *"there is a possibility that power equipment could lose functions if a 14-meter-high tsunami hits the Fukushima plant, with seawater flowing inside the (reactor) turbine buildings"* (Kyodo News, 2012). NISA officials saw no need of action *"because a total power failure was not seen as an imminent threat"* (Sunaoshi et al., 2012). On March 11, 2011 Japan was hit by a magnitude 9 earthquake, which was followed by several tsunamis with a maximum height of 38.9 meters (IAEA Expert Mission, 2011). 20,896 lives were lost (USGS, 2012). The combined catastrophe led to a long-lasting, complete power loss at the Fukushima Daiichi nuclear station which resulted in a meltdown at three of six reactor units as well as a hydrogen explosion at reactor nos. 1, 3 and 4 (Masaya, 2012). This was the second INES 7 accident in history.[2]

1.1 Background and Motivation

The Fukushima meltdown is one of many disastrous events that can be attributed to unexplainably optimistic forecasts. In April 2010, the petrol company BP had no effective method to stop the oil leak caused by the explosion of their offshore drilling

---

[2] The first mayor accident (INES 7) happened in 1986 in Chernobyl, Ukraine. INES 7 is the highest category of nuclear disasters with severe impact on people and environment (IAEA, 2010).

platform *Deepwater Horizon* in the Gulf of Mexico. There was no worst-case scenario plan because it was considered costly and unlikely to happen (Steinberg, 2011). Similar behavior can be seen on a number of other occasions such as the Bhopal disaster in 1984.[3] The public seems to be aware of the human misjudgment but fails to prevent it. One reason might be that, although scientists have contributed a lot to understanding the nature of overconfidence, there are still some "blank spots on the map". The interdisciplinary field of behavioral economics is younger than the established neo-classical approach and requires further long-term investigation to understand all aspects and conditions of irrationality in economical behavior. This research examines whether there is a statistically provable connection between the level of overconfidence and the educational achievement in a certain school system. Due to the given framework of this paper, it was not possible to extend the research to several international systems. Nevertheless, the outcome should help prevent the harmful aspects of overconfidence. It aims to support the development of a suitable strategy against future misjudgments.

Before continuing with an explanation of the research methodology, a detailed definition of overconfidence is needed. Due to the importance of this word, the terminology discussion is part of the first chapter.

1.2 Definition: Overconfidence

There are several definitions of overconfidence in the standard literature. They all follow the basic idea of irrational behavior and its roots in psychology. With even the first research in this field, scholars have been able to prove irrationality in decision making. In an experiment the test subjects were given two scenarios (A and B) each with two choices:

(A) *Would you prefer $ 100 today or $ 110 tomorrow?*
(B) *Would you prefer $ 100 thirty days from now or $ 110 thirty-one days from now?*

Many subjects gave different answers for A and B (Diamond and Vartiainen, 2007). This shows an inconsistent and irrational decision-making process and conflicts with

---

[3] For further information about the toxic contamination of the Indian city of Bhopal caused by a chemical explosion see: (Bryan, 2003)

the neo-classical view and the idea of rational decision makers, who should always behave in their best interest given all relevant information and their own preferences.[4] In that experiment, all subjects should have chosen the same answer for A and B. A completely rational person would have calculated the present value (PV) for both scenarios at the exact same discount rate.[5]

As mentioned before, overconfidence is one factor that can explain such irrational behavior. The following terminology is designed to establish a suitable hypothesis as well as to support the empirical research.[6] The phenomenon is commonly referred to as the overestimation of one's own abilities, knowledge, and future prospects, but it does not occur as one single bias (Barber and Odean, 2001). Numerous psychological mechanisms lead to overconfidence. They will be defined separately and will be discussed in a final overview.

1.2.1 Unrealistic Optimism

Too rosy expectations are closely linked to other relevant biases in this chapter. The effect can be described as an overestimation of the likelihood of a desirable event to happen or the prediction of a future event to be more positive than it will be (Müller, 2007). Unrealistic optimism can be both a cause and a consequence of overconfidence. If an investor is too optimistic about the future price increase of a certain stock, he will not be able to consider that a decrease in value is equally possible. His bright expectation convinces him that his actions will lead to further gains. In that case, unrealistic optimism serves as a heuristic[7] and causes overconfidence. If, however, a couple is absolutely sure about their ability to maintain a stable marriage, their overconfidence and unrealistic optimism will lead them to disregard the chance of being one out of three couples that divorce.

---

[4] These standards follow the model of "Homo economicus". For a short overview and criticism see: (Krugman, 2007)
[5] The PV shows the value of future inflows at the time of investment. For detailed information see: (Tietze, 2011)
[6] Other concepts and criticism are presented in chapter 4.
[7] In behavioral science a heuristic is a short decision-making process that excludes some relevant information and/or stochastic facts.

1.2.2 Better-Than-Average Effect

The BTAE is a major component of overconfidence. In many cases, people use their own characteristics as benchmark for others. This is either caused by a lack of alternatives or by an undefined peer group. When subjects have to rank their performance, they frequently state it is above average compared to their peers (Guenther, 2009).[8] In a well-known study Svenson could prove the BTAE by asking subjects to assess their driving skills. 77% of the participating Swedish drivers felt that they drive safer than average (Benoit and Dubra, 2009). Although this would be desirable, it is impossible. The majority cannot be above average. This bias is closely connected to the representativeness heuristic. People have a systematic misconception about probabilities and distribution (Kahneman et al., 1982).

The flattering self-evaluation leads to overconfidence, because decisions are made under the impression of an unrealistic assessment of one's own capabilities. A startup owner who thinks that his management skills are above average could ignore important business actions of his competitors which might have a negative impact on his own company.

1.2.3 Illusion of Control

The concept of the IOC describes the human belief of being able to have an influence on random future events. When IOC is present, people are more likely to take risks. In an often-cited experiment subjects *"participated in a lottery where they had choice or no choice of a familiar or unfamiliar lottery ticket"*. Then they had an opportunity to exchange their ticket with a ticket from a lottery with better odds, namely, a lottery with a smaller amount of tickets to be drawn from (Harvey et al., 1978). Clearly all subjects should have taken advantage of this opportunity to increase their chance of winning, but it turned out that precisely those with a chosen or familiar ticket rejected the offer. IOC made them believe they would be better off with their first choice.

Furthermore, IOC is present if the outcome not only depends on luck but also involves a certain skill level (Grömminger, 2011). Poker and roulette are examples of

---

[8] Researchers found out that the phenomenon increases on questions regarding moral or subjectively construed characteristics.

skill and luck. It has been shown that poker players systematically underestimate the role of luck in their game (Shead et al., 2008). Extrinsic incentives such as money or other rewards fuel the IOC. In their absence, only subjects with a high desire of control acted according to previous tests with money incentives (Burger and Schnerring, 1982). The illusion of having control over uncertain events leads to overconfident decisions. While a rational thought process would include the possibility of a negative or positive outcome, an IOC-biased decision making process underestimates the chance of an undesired result or even completely ignores it. A good example is a private investor who mistakenly believes that his own selecting of stocks will automatically lead to higher future profit than stocks selected by anybody else. In this case, the IOC is responsible for his overconfidence.

1.2.4 Illusion of Knowledge

There is a common belief about the connection between the amount of information available and the quality of decisions made. The more input a person gets, the better his judgment will be (Schwartz, 2005). Scientists found that in many cases exactly the reverse is true. In an experiment subjects were asked to predict the results of randomly chosen National Basketball Association (NBA) games of one season. They received statistics about the teams' records and halftime scores. In addition, half of all participants were told the team names (eg. Dallas Mavericks vs. Chicago Bulls) while the others did not know these names (Team A vs. Team B). Basketball fans insist that knowledge of team names will increase accuracy of their prediction because they are able to connect the information with other significant facts about each team (e.g. injuries). The study showed that the opposite happened. Participants with the additional cues relied less on statistical odds. They bet on more familiar teams and earned on average less than those without the team names (Hall et al., 2007). This phenomenon is called illusion of knowledge.

The core message is that additional information does not ultimately lead to higher accuracy in decision making. Even though our cognitive system needs a certain amount of knowledge to make a decision, more knowledge goes along with a higher confidence level but not better judgment. This is called the *"less-is-more effect"*. Similar findings were made when the available knowledge exceeded the required amount of information (Iyengar and Lepper, 2000). This can be referred to as the *"more-is-less effect"* (Hall et al., 2007). This is the reason why experts are affected by the overconfidence bias. Their specific knowledge increases their confidence level but not their accuracy.

In several experiments aiming to test the illusion of knowledge, participants showed clear signs of overconfidence in their decision-making progress.[9] They were more likely to take risks and ignore significant statistical cues. A doctor who is convinced that his in-depth medical knowledge will automatically help him to find an appropriate cure for a certain illness might oversee important aspects which occur less frequently. In such cases, the illusion of knowledge is a major driving force for overconfidence.

1.2.5 Self-serving bias

The SSB is a special cognitive process that serves as an internal protection mechanism of a person's self-esteem. The validity of harmful influences resulting from negative feedback are changed or rejected. The bias puts the focus on strengths and achievements and suppresses failures and repercussions. It *"internalizes success and externalizes failure"* (Sherrill, 2007). In laboratory tests participants had to complete certain tasks either alone, in pairs or groups. Some individuals, pairs or groups received positive feedback after they had finished their tasks, while the work of others was assessed as a failure. In the end, subjects had to evaluate the outcome of their efforts. Those told that they had failed attributed performance to external factors such as misfortune, degree of difficulty or the interference of others. Participants who received positive feedback stated that the outcome was mainly caused by internal factors such as ability or intelligence (Campbell and Sedikides, 1999).

Researchers connect the SSB with unrealistic optimism. People usually expect positive future events. They think they will *"pass tests, get good jobs, and have long-lasting relationships rather than fail, get fired, or divorce"* (Sherrill, 2007). The frequent illusion of success causes overconfidence. They do not expect a negative outcome because, in their imagination, it has hardly ever happened before. This qualifies the SSB as the most important reason for overconfidence. An employee

---

[9] For example in (Bank and Kottke, 2005) or (Hall et al., 2007)

who is frequently late to work, often sick and works inaccurately will not blame himself for his non-performance because his cognitive self-serving process suggests that all that happened is due to external factors.

1.2.6 Summary

As stated at the beginning of 1.2, overconfidence is described as the combination of overestimation of one's own abilities, knowledge, and future prospects as well as underestimation or ignorance of possible failure. The heuristic is influenced or intensified by several cognitive or perceptual processes – the five most important are explained above. The effects of overconfidence on behavior and decision making are varied, and a decrease in risk aversion and wrong calibration are just two examples.[10]

Table 1 summarizes the five most important processes that are closely connected with overconfidence.

Figure 1: Five Factors of Overconfidence

(Complied by the author)

---

[10] Wrong calibration can be seen in the choice of an overly-narrow confidence interval if the question cannot be answered directly. This effect is important as it will be tested in the student survey to determine the overconfidence level and eventual differences among several school types. Further explanation can be found in chapter 2 and 5.

1.3 Structure

At the end of this chapter the structure of the research paper is described. The following section, chapter 2, describes the workflow of the centerpiece of this study. A clear overview of how the data was collected and assessed is given. A detailed explanation of the school system where the tests took place follows. Chapter 3 describes the test environment and its limitation and covers the differences in the German education system in various states and the influence of the Bologna Process. Chapter 4 is a review of the literature characterizing overconfidence and explaining criticism of the concept. The fifth chapter begins with a research hypothesis and introduces the empirical part of this paper. The process of the data collection, the findings of the study and the interpretation are also included in this section. Chapter 6 includes the conclusion and discussion of the impact and limitation of the results.

2 METHODOLOGY

As mentioned in chapter 1, this study aims to test whether there is a statistically provable difference between the level of overconfidence and a person's education. Therefore, a questionnaire was designed to test students' miscalibration in several steps.[11] The questionnaire includes ten questions which should be answered first directly and then within a 90% confidence interval (CI). An example was given to explain the procedure. In addition, it was remarked that each question had to be answered without the assistance of other participants or technical devices such as smartphones or laptop computers. Finally, subjects were prompted to state their age, gender, current level of education, and their aspired degree. These data were required to group all subjects correctly in order to test if there is a difference.

In the first step, the questionnaire was handed out to teachers from all basic school types in Southern Germany. The teachers were then advised to give the questionnaire to their ninth graders as well as to observe the experiment. The ninth grade is the last year of compulsory school in Germany and therefore the only choice for a study seeking results from all levels of education. The PISA test, conducted by the OECD,

---

[11] The original questionnaire can be found in the appendix on page B. It was modified to a smaller scale. The actual font size was 12 and can be seen on the research disc attached to this paper. The translated version is on page A. The English questionnaire was not used for research purposes and is only provided for reader's convenience.

surveys the same group of students and shows that they are able to understand the questions.[12] As there were no extrinsic incentives for participation, the questionnaire was designed to have an intrinsic interest. The teachers received the answers and sources of all ten questions and were advised to tell their students the correct answers after all of the questionnaires had been collected.[13] This way the subjects received immediate feedback. The pretest showed that the subjects had the impression of participating in an interesting exercise rather than in a psychological study.[14] It is important to mention that neither the questionnaire nor the answer sheet gave any indication of the aim or the topic of the study. All participating students thought it was about their ability to estimate the correct answer. However, this is partly true because their metaknowledge was subliminally tested.[15] Earlier research showed that participants will behave differently if they are aware that the aim of the study is to test their confidence level (Mayrhofer, 2006).

In the second step, the same questionnaire was given to several teachers from a vocational school as well as to teachers from a specialized secondary school (SSS).[16] They were advised to give the survey to students from classes with different educational backgrounds. All students had either a General Certificate of Secondary Education (The German Mittlere Reife; ISCED 2) or a General Certificate for University Entrance (The German Abitur, Austrian Matura; ISCED 3A).[17] This step was to determine if the results obtained from the ninth graders are consistent with the result from older students with the same educational background and first work experience.

In the third and last step, the same questionnaire was handed out to undergraduates in an electrical engineering degree program at a technical university. This last test was

---

[12] For more information about PISA see: (OECD, 2012)
[13] The original answer sheet can be found in the appendix on page D. It was modified to a smaller scale. The English translation is on page C.
[14] Chapter 5 describes the pretest and its impact on the survey.
[15] While common knowledge comprehends facts and details, metaknowledge represents the human understanding of nature and its limits. It helps a person to know what he does not know. If a man calls a plumber after a green breakage, he admits that his knowledge of plumbing is not enough to fix the problem. In that case his metaknowledge helped him to realize that the task would exceed his common knowledge.
[16] All school types which have been used for the survey will be explained in chapter 3.
[17] The International Standard Classification of Education (ISCED) is part of the next chapter.

carried out to determine whether the trend of step one and two continues. It is certain that all students have a university entrance certificate.

Finally, every questionnaire received a unique number and all data were collected in SPSS®. The scanned questionnaires, data sets and calculations are available upon request.[18] This guarantees complete transparency and eliminates a need for recalculation. The procedure of data analysis is explained in chapter 5. The next section will cover the educational level aspect of this thesis.

3 THE GERMAN EDUCATION SYSTEM

According to Article 26 of the 1948 Universal Declaration of Human Rights education is a fundamental right (Spring, 2000). It has been described as *"a process of teaching, training and learning, especially in schools or colleges, to improve knowledge and develop skills"* (*Oxford Advanced Learner's Dictionary of Current English*, 2005). Germany is a federal republic and education is a responsibility of its federal states. Therefore, there are 16 slightly different forms of one basic system. The following figure explains the conceptual framework.

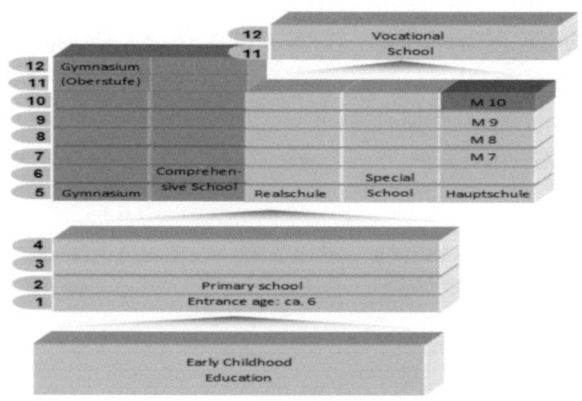

Figure 2: German Education System

(Complied by the author)

---

[18] Contact: stud.Dominik.Piehlmaier@fh-kufstein.ac.at

All of the slightly different school forms have the three certificates of secondary education in common. After the ninth grade, there is a possibility of receiving the Qualifying Lower Secondary General Education Certificate (the German Qualifizierte Hauptschulabschluss; ISCED 2). One year later, students have a chance of acquiring the GCSE and, two years after that, the GCUE. Since 1997, the UNESCO has provided a standardized concept for these educational achievements to ease the interpretation and significance of a local certificate on a global scale (UNESCO, 1997). The acquisition of the German certificates is subject to obtaining positive results in the final exams.[19] These tests are different in every state and the equivalency is not guaranteed. The annual school report shows that students in the south of the republic score higher than their counterparts in the north. In particular Bavaria has a competitive school system which contributes to its being the ranking leader among the 16 states (Bavarian State Government, 2003). This is the reason why the field study was conducted in Southern Germany, and also why it is important to mention the federal differences between the basic German school system and the Bavarian concept.

3.1 Federal Differences

The fundamental distinction is the separation of the various secondary schools. There is no comprehensive school in Bavaria. This, at first view, might curb social mobility but there are educational paths which connect each school type and allow mobility. It is possible, although not easy, for a student of a lower secondary school (e.g. Hauptschule) to receive the GCUE in order to be able to study at a university. Pupils holding a GCSE have numerous ways to obtain the entrance certificate. Immediately following the tenth grade, they can complete the last two years at the highest secondary school (Gymnasium). Alternatively, they may also continue their education in social studies, technology or business at the SSS (Fachoberschule). Another possibility is to continue at an upper vocational school (Berufsoberschule) which requires a completed apprenticeship and a vocational certificate. This is a typical combination in the German dual education system, which connects professional training with

---

[19] There is one exception: Students from the highest secondary school (German Gynasium) receive the GCSE automatically after they have passed the tenth grade.

vocational learning at a vocational school (Berufsschule). Figure 3 explains the various paths and possibilities in contrast to the basic system which was charted on page 11.

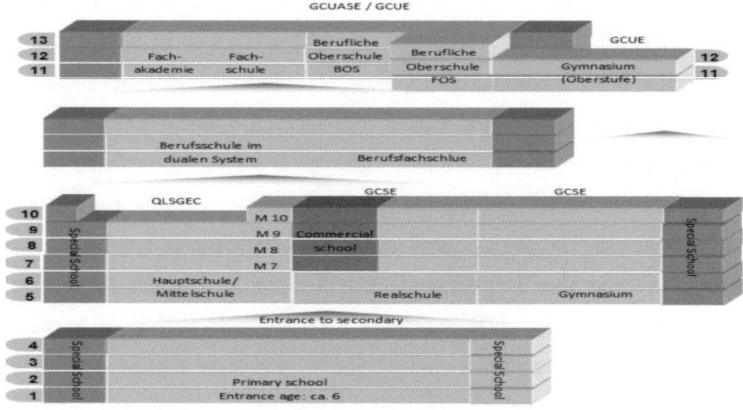

Figure 3: Bavarian Education System

(Complied by the author based on Bavarian Ministry of Education)

As mentioned before, the Bavarian system is competitive and the annual failure rate is rather high. On average, 6.1% of all Bavarian Gymansium students fail to make the grade, about one-third of them change to a lower secondary school (Hackl, 2004). Those who obtain the entrance certificate have basically two options. They can study in Germany at a university or a UAS or study abroad. Most students stay in Europe and benefit from the Bologna Process and its European Credit Transfer and Accumulation System. The next subitem will explain the reform and its impact on this research.

3.2 Influences of the Bologna Process

On 19 June 1999, the European Ministers of Education published a joint declaration to implement the *"European Higher Education Area"* (Campbell and Van der Wende, 2000). The official announcement is also called the Bologna Declaration and started the corresponding process. Its predefined aims were mainly to introduce bachelor, master, and doctorate studies instead of many different national university degrees. In addition, the purpose of the reforms was to provide a *"quality assurance"* and to guarantee *"recognition of qualifications and periods of study"* (European Commission, 2011). The official launch of the Higher Education Area was more than 10 years later on March 11/12 2010 in Budapest and Vienna. The ministers and the commission expected the reform to be an incentive to increase student mobility. It was one attempt to decrease the long-term European unemployment rate by taking first steps towards a common European labor market. The idea was to implement policies which would lead to higher student mobility resulting in an increase in labor mobility in the future.

In 2009 the Eurobarometer showed that, although one-third of all students planned to study abroad, the majority did not want to participate in a higher education exchange program. 41% never planned to study in a foreign country and 11% gave up their plan to go abroad (The Gallup Organization, 2009). Nevertheless, a combination of the Erasmus Student Mobility Program and the Bologna Process shows a clear, upward trend in student mobility:[20]

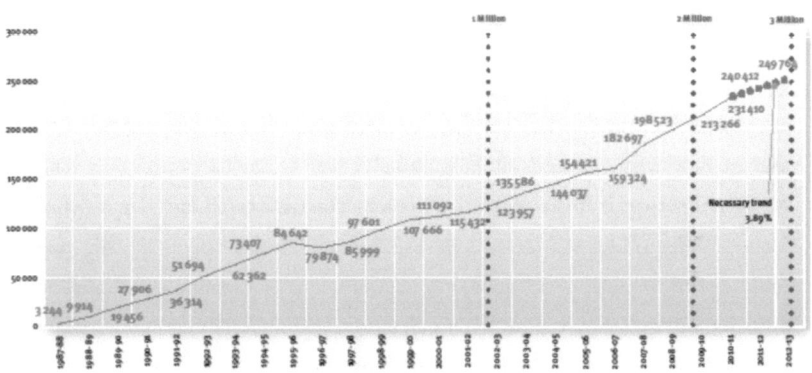

Figure 4: Development of Erasmus Students per Year

(Source: Erasmus - Facts, Figures & Trends)

As shown in Figure 4, there were 231,410 students studying in another European country in 2010-11. This represents an annual increase of 8.5% compared to the previous year (European Commission, 2012).

---

[20] The Erasmus Program started in the academic year of 1987-88. It was designed to ease the bureaucratic procedure of an exchange semester and to give those students a financial support. Especially the bureaucratic aspect was later replaced by the ECTS in the Bologna Process.

This is an important consideration since the research includes university students.[21] Degree programs are not as homogeneous as school classes. There are students from various countries with a different educational and cultural background. As stated above, the Bologna Process abets the student mobility in Europe and, therefore increases the chance of heterogeneous subjects in tertiary education. The next chapter reviews the literature and explains why previous studies in this field suggest that this might lead to variance inflation in this particular subgroup.

4 REVIEW OF LITERATURE

Overconfidence is a *distortion of judgment* which has been tested in various experiments although the knowledge of its presence is not new. In the 19th century, the economist and philosopher John Stuart Mill wrote *"that any opinion of which they [mankind] feel very certain may be one of the examples of the error to which they acknowledge themselves to be liable"* (Russo and Schoemaker, 1992).

Many different explanations and concepts of overconfidence can be found in the relevant literature. Camerer and Lovallo (1999) describe it as the overestimation of one's own relative abilities compared to a peer group. The authors state that whenever people have to assess their position in a distribution they are likely to rate it above average especially regarding positive attributes such as income prospects or longevity. This, however, is impossible in a symmetrically distributed trait. Their definition focuses on the BTAE and includes the aspect of an unreasonably optimistic view on future events. Brenner et al. (2004) say that most studies examine overconfidence in a situation of uncertainty in which a judgment is required. In those cases, irrational behavior manifests itself in non-regressive predictions and overly-narrow confidence intervals. This is an important perception because the student questionnaire on page A tests whether it is also true if subjects do not have to think about their degree of confidence for each individual question, but rather the width of their interval on pseudo common knowledge questions.[22] The study tested students' metaknowledge and the possible differences between the various school types.

---

[21] A list of participating schools and institutes can be found in the appendix on page F.
[22] The average ninth grader does not know the length of Greenland's coast and the students are not expected to. They were asked to estimate the answers. Most questions cannot be seen as common but

Studies which focus on irrational behavior on financial markets state that *"human beings are overconfident about their abilities, their knowledge, and their future prospects"* (Barber and Odean, 2001). Biased investors sell and buy more frequently, they apply risky stock-picking methods and follow guru advices (Shiller, 2000). These traders invest more time and money to gather information about their stocks and the market (Barber and Odean, 2001). They influenced by the illusions of knowledge and control because they think that additional information helps them to increase their profits. Similarly, they believe that the stocks they buy will do better than average.[23] Financial market participants tend to disinvest in stocks which experience further price increases after they sold them. At the same time, they keep those that constantly decline because they do not want to realize their losses (Shefrin, 2002).

Daniel et al. (2001) suggest that individuals are especially confident about private information. They overestimate its precision and overreact accordingly. Overconfidence could not be detected in cases where the trader did not have such information. Overestimation of one's own abilities and positive future events seems to be a common problem in almost all professions. Previous experiments testing physicians and nurses, investment bankers, engineers, entrepreneurs, lawyers, negotiators, and managers showed that the heuristic influences their decision-making process (Barber and Odean, 2001). In his often-cited research Oskamp (1965) gave 32 psychologists and psychology students a case study based on real medical records. The case was divided in 4 sections and every subject was asked to answer 25 specific questions about the case after reading each section. They also had to provide their confidence level on how certain they were that the given response was correct. The surprising results showed that the average final accuracy was less than 28% with no significant changes over the four stages. However, the confidence rose significantly from 33% at Stage 1 to 53% at the end of Stage 4. Though the results cannot be generalized, the study is still a good example of overconfidence and illusion of knowledge among experts.

---

rather as specific. That is why it is called pseudo common knowledge questions. Further details will follow in chapter 5.
[23] See subitem 1.2.3 and 1.2.4 on pages 5, 6.

4.1 Confounders of Overconfidence

It is due to the complexity of the human cognitive system that a bias does not occur at the same intensity in every single person. There are various determinants that can influence overconfidence. This section contains the five most important factors and describes them as confounders to the heuristic. They can have a positive and negative impact on a person's confidence level. Furthermore, they bias the outcome of a statistical calculation in one particular direction. For each subitem there will be an explanation of how to avoid a misinterpretation of the final results caused by the factor itself.

4.1.1   Gender

The overestimation of one's own abilities is part of human nature but, on average, men are more affected than women. Barber and Odean (2001) showed that male investors trade more than their female counterparts and by doing so, they adversely affect their performance. Barber and Odean stated that a rational investor only trades if the expected return exceeds the costs of the transaction, such as taxes and commission. An overconfident trader overestimates the accuracy of his information and thereby the expected return. The authors said that people may even trade when the true expected net gain does not result in breaking even. However, the gender difference is not universal; it depends on the task. Lundeberg et al. (1994) said that the gap between the male and female confidence level is bigger in typically masculine areas. The finance industry is one area where men are disproportionally represented. The specific domains are also known for their lack of clear and immediate feedback, which therefore also increases overconfidence. Whenever unambiguous feedback is available without delay, the gender differences disappear (Barber and Odean, 2001).

This research contains no masculine tasks. The pseudo common knowledge questions do not favor a specific gender. They are equally hard to answer for both male and female students. The analysis contains different groups, also for men and women, and all subjects received immediate feedback after the test. The detection of a gender difference is discussed in chapter 5.

4.1.2 Age

Common sense says that older people are better in judging their estimations. They have a sound metaknowledge after a lifetime of decision making in various forms and situations. This social group knows what it does not know and therefore knows the limits of its knowledge. Kovalchik et al. (2005) followed this argumentation. In their study, they formed two groups with 51 junior college students and 50 highly educated, neurologically healthy seniors aged from 70 to 95. The authors tested their confidence level by giving each subject a questionnaire with 20 trivia questions. All questions had two possible answers. Participants were instructed to select an answer and then provide a confidence assessment of their choice. The lowest possible assessment was 50% rising in increments of tens up to 100. The older group did slightly better on the test and showed a lower level of overconfidence. This suggests that age has a positive impact on self-evaluation.

Hershey and Wilson (1997) tested 28 undergraduate students and 32 university alumni with an average age of 71.1 years. About half of each group's participants were trained, the other half untrained. The scholars created subgroups and examined their behavior on six questions concerning financial planning for retirement. After completing these problems, subjects had to rate the quality of their answers on a Likert-scale ranging from 1 (very poor solution) to 7 (very good solution). The findings revealed that *"the absolute magnitude of errors made by older participants were equivalent to those made by younger ones"*. A clear connection between age and overconfidence was not visible. Crawford and Stankov (1996) drew a reversed picture. They stated that *"older subjects showed a consistent tendency towards greater overconfidence compared to younger subjects"*.

This shows that, so far, scholars have not been able to prove a significant correlation between age and confidence level which might be representative for the whole population. The connection remains task-dependent and inconsistent. Due to these aspects and the fact that the age difference among the tested students is by far not as large as in the above mentioned research, age difference is considered as a minor determinant in this paper

4.1.3 Mental Health

A sane neurological and cognitive system is another important aspect of overconfidence. It can be seen as a prerequisite because overestimation of one's own abilities protects our self-esteem from threat and injury. Campbell and Sedikides (1999) tell the story of a psychology student called Lence and his reaction to self-threat. Lence got a bad grade on his midterm exam. Instead of admitting his failure he blamed external factors. His instructor graded harshly and he couldn't sleep the night before the test. Although the student realized he got a bad mark, his ego stayed untouched. He rejected the validity of the negative outcome and denied his share of the responsibility for it.

These situations are familiar to most human beings. Sherrill (2007) states *"that a number of cognitive, motivational, and psychological factors combine to create"* this protection mechanism, but it does not work for everyone. Individuals who suffer from depression or chronically low self-esteem tend to internalize failure and externalize success. They overestimate their weaknesses and underrate their abilities. The SSB has no or only little effect on this group. This leads to a process of adjustments in their confidence level because their ego cannot be protected from negative feedback. Calibration studies result in a phenomenon called underconfidence. Their accuracy, which is usually the percentage of right answers, exceeds the stated confidence level. While mentally healthy people rarely decrease their overconfidence the reverse is true for depressed individuals.

Mental health plays an important role in analyzing the heuristic. It is possible that the data includes students suffering from a mental illness. Underconfidence occurs only in rare situations or under certain conditions. [24] Every case of accuracy > 90% confidence, which means 10 out of 10 right answers, will be assessed in order to determine if mental health could be the cause.

4.1.4 Euphoria

The distortion of judgment is not exclusively a mental aspect. It can also be provoked by biochemical processes. Russo and Schoemaker (1992) suggest that adrenalin and

---

[24] Subitem 4.2 gives further details on other conditions of underconfidence.

endorphins, which are responsible for strong emotions, may lead to overconfidence. The decision-making process under the influence of euphoria can be biased. Overconfident actions are more likely to happen after an event of personal or professional success. The consumption of alcohol and drugs can have the same effect. The authors provide an example of the Ford Motor Company and their experience with introducing a suggestion system which led to a tremendous euphoria within their workforce. The top management had to impose a cooling-off period before the implementation of any given suggestion. The risk of rashly made decisions was simply too high.

Although it became clear that euphoria can be a confounder of overconfidence, it is not expected to influence the result of this research. There is no evidence that the questionnaire, with its 10 pseudo common knowledge questions, provokes strong biochemical processes. During the observed pre-test, there were no signs of euphoria among participants.

4.1.5   Education

The link between education and overestimation of one's own capabilities is the quintessence of this research. Yates et at. (1996) argued that there are cultural differences in overconfidence. Asian students tend to be more affected than their American counterparts. The authors saw a connection to the different school systems and their applied teaching method. Ex-cathedra teaching that focuses on rote learning fuels overconfidence. These are widely-used teaching methods in many traditional Asian school systems and may therefore explain the differences. One reason is that many of these countries have languages with thousands of characters which have to be internalized by all students. Li et al. (2006) substantiated the previous findings. They tested 316 university students from Singapore and 340 from Mainland China. All students were ethnical Chinese and had the same cultural background. The striking difference was the education system. Singapore adopted a more westernized model, whereas China retained its traditional method of learning. All subjects had to answer the same peer-comparison problem. The result confirmed that Chinese students exhibit a higher degree of overconfidence than their Singaporean counterparts.

These findings stress the importance of the Bologna Process to this paper. It is not the cultural difference that influences a person's confidence level, but his educational background. The reforms incentivized student mobility and created more heterogeneous degree programs. Figure 4 on page 14 shows the steady increase of exchange students. This development is the reason why it is more likely that the study contains university students from various school systems. The single choice question about the highest reached level of education is crucial to address this specific confounder.[25] Participants' answers were used to create subgroups in order to minimize the harmful effect of a heterogeneous group on the standard deviation.

4.2 Criticism

The universal existence of overconfidence is not without controversy among scholars. Although dozens of studies showed its impact on human behavior, critics say that most results were generated by calibration tests (Brenner et al., 2004). They state that the overly-narrow CI is, to a large extent, produced by the selection of difficult or misleading questions. Brenner et al. (2004) gave a common example of a standard calibration study, *"Which city is further north: Rome or New York?"*. The fact that the right answer is Rome surprises most people. The majority is convinced that New York is further north and they will therefore state a high confidence level for their answer. In addition, critics say that these problems are not *"a representative sample from the knowledge domain"*. Brenner et al. (2004) could prove that overconfidence persists even if the questions were chosen completely random. Furthermore, they showed that difficulty plays an important role. There is a strong positive correlation between the degree of difficulty of a question and a subject's confidence level. This phenomenon is called the difficulty effect (also the hard-easy effect). If the difficulty is low, underconfidence will appear. The reason is that while accuracy increases, confidence remains at about the same level.

Benoît and Dubra (2009) argue that overconfidence may be just an illusion. The authors focus on the BTAE and differentiate between *"work that proceeds by means of questionnaires and work that asks subjects to take actions"*. Using Bayes's rule

---

[25] It is important to underline that the English version of the questionnaire was not used at any time for the data ascertainment. Subjects could only choose between German (or Austrian) certificates. This was done on purpose to detect statistical outliers more easily.

they suggest that the majority can rate themselves above average by considering all available information.[26] Benoît and Dubra conclude that *"much of the supposed evidence for overconfidence does not indicate overconfidence at all"*. The criticism was considered for designing the questionnaire and conducting the study. Benoît and Dubra's work has little impact on this paper as subjects did not have to compare their answers or abilities to a defined or undefined peer group. Even if people used Bayes's rule in their daily life, the BTAE is by definition only one driver of overconfidence. It is not used as a synonym in this paper. In addition, it is questionable whether Bayes's fundamental rule has such an important impact on decision making under uncertainty (El-Gamal and Grether, 1995). The ten questions were purposely created to be very difficult to answer but not misleading. Students should realize that there is little chance to answer these problems correctly. In fact, they should realize that a wide CI is needed in order to be 90% sure that their answer lies somewhere in between. As mentioned before, Brenner et al. (2004) suggest that this tends to increase overconfidence. The aim of this study is not to prove the existence of this heuristic, but to test whether the confidence level varies between the different school types. All students had exactly the same questionnaire. If the difficulty of questions raises overconfidence, it will bias every subject in the same direction. Furthermore, the confidence level of 90% was given. This is contrary to other calibration tests because, generally, people have problems stating their confidence in percent. Most participants find it hard to differentiate between, e.g. 60 and 70% confidence. A 90% CI, however, commonly represents a strong confidence but not certainty. In addition, the questionnaire included a best guess. Russo and Schoemaker (1992) call this a psychological anchor. People do not want to move too far away from their first estimate. The authors showed that this behavior fuels overconfidence. The reason why it is still part of the test is that ninth graders are not used to stating their thoughts in intervals. The best guess gives them a chance to think about the question before they have to provide an interval. If it anchors, every subject will be affected. Therefore, the differences between the school types will not change.

---

[26] The paper assumes that people use Bayes's fundamental rule to estimate their probabilities in uncertain situations. A basic overview on how to apply Bayes's rule see ("Lecture 4: Conditional Probability, Total Probability, Bayes's Rule," 2005).

The next chapter discusses the empirical research. It gives a research hypothesis which includes all findings of the previous sections. Chapter 5 explains the process of data collection and shows its findings. It ends with an interpretation of the results.

5 EMPIRICAL RESEARCH

The diagnosis of miscalibration among participants is the most important aspect of the data analysis since it fundamental to compare the different overconfidence levels. The 90% CI represent 9 correct answers within 10 stated intervals. If a participant answers less or more than 9 questions correctly, he is by definition miscalibrated. His CI is either too narrow or too wide. A calibrated subject answers exactly 9 out of 10 questions correctly. His accuracy (A) equals the CI.

5.1 Hypothesis

Mathematically, overconfidence *"is defined as the difference between mean confidence and overall accuracy"* (Brenner et al., 2004). It is necessary to detect overconfidence in order to test the hypothesis. If A_x is the accuracy of subject x from group y, then the average accuracy of all participants from group y is $\mu_y = \frac{A_1 + A_2 + \cdots + A_n}{n}$

If	Then the group is on average
$\mu_y < 9$	overconfident
$\mu_y = 9$	calibrated
$\mu_y > 9$	underconfident

There are three groups of ninth graders in the first step. Those who want to get their QLSGEC (μ_1), the GCSE (μ_2), or the GCUE (μ_3).[27] The vast majority has not yet received a leaving certificate. The basic question is if pupils from these three school types show different behavior in a situation of uncertainty, namely, a statistically significant difference in their average accuracy compared to the given level of confidence. The following hypothesis will help to answer this question. The confidence coefficient is 95% ($\alpha=5\%$) and constant for every test.

---

[27] The numbers are consistent with the code plan in the appendix on page F. This code plan was used to analyze the data in SPSS®.

H_0: $\mu_1=\mu_2=\mu_3$ $\qquad$ H_1: $\mu_1 \neq \mu_2 \neq \mu_3$

H_0 says that there is no difference in accuracy between the three secondary school types. This means that the students are no more or less overconfident than all other ninth graders because the confidence level of 90% was predefined. H_1 states that there is a variation in any direction.

The second step compares the average accuracy of students from a vocational school and a SSS.[28] All students have at least one leaving certificate.[29] Those with a GCSE ($\mu_{2;0}$; VM-Classes) are about the same age, but there are also vocational students with a GCUASE or a GCUE($\mu_{4;0}$; VA-Classes). They are in separate classes and their results will be compared to schoolmates holding a GCSE. The test is relevant to this study for two reasons: It will reveal if the picture drawn in step 1 continues and if a first work experience changes students' decision-making process. All tested vocational students have an apprenticeship in the insurance industry. Their counterparts from the SSS do not have formal work experience and continued school in order to obtain the GCUASE or the GCUE ($\mu_{2;4}$). The hypothesis is as follows:

H_0: $\mu_{2;0}=\mu_{4;0}=\mu_{2;4}$ $\qquad$ H_1: $\mu_{2;0} \neq \mu_{4;0} \neq \mu_{2;4}$

H_0 says that there is no difference in the average accuracy between vocational students with a GCSE, a GCUASE/GCUE, and SSS students. H_1 states the reverse. The results will be compared to those from step 1.

The last step tests how the heuristic affects calibration of tertiary education students. Universities request a GCUE ($\mu_{4;5}$) and put their focus on scientific research. Only students of the highest secondary school (Gymnasium) who obtain an entrance certificate can enter university directly. If the level of education in years or quality matters, there should be a significant difference between Gymnasiums ninth graders and TUM undergraduates studying at the highest ranked university in Germany (ShanghaiRanking Consultancy, 2011). Therefore, a suitable hypothesis is:

H_0: $\mu_3=\mu_{4;5}$ $\qquad$ H_1: $\mu_3 \neq \mu_{4;5}$

---

[28] The vocational degree is part of the German dual education system and is not directly included in the secondary education path. Therefore, the degree was coded with 0.
[29] It is necessary to enlarge the labels of the groups' average accuracy to distinguish between the various leaving certificates. This was not the case during the first step as students did not have any leaving certificates yet.

The null hypothesis suggests the same confidence level for Gymnasium students and TUM undergraduates. The alternative hypothesis says that there is a positive or negative discrepancy between those two groups.

In addition to the three main hypotheses, there were several other tests in the analyses. They all refer to previous findings in this field which are described in chapter 4. The data was used to determine a possible gender gap and age differences in subjects' level of overconfidence. The Bavarian commercial school pupils were compared to their Realschule counterparts in North Rhine-Westphalia (NRW). This is of special interest because both groups aim for the same leaving certificate but NRW just introduced the comprehensive school. The tested ninth graders were usual Realschule students and former Hauptschule pupils. This comparison might also provide evidence if the results can be valid for Germany as a whole.

5.2 Process of Primary Data Collection

The beginning of the data collection was a pretest at BMW Financial Services. The test consists of a heterogeneous group of 21 subjects from various departments. There were 12 females and 9 males with a different educational background. All forms were valid. The feedback led to a change in the layout. Participants said that the introduction was too long and they hardly read it. A passage was integrated to separate the introduction from the example. Furthermore people misunderstood the "current target level of education". They stated their long-term goal instead of the current target. The word "current" was bold to increase the legibility. There were no further changes. The pretest forms were not used for the data analysis.[30] As for the whole collection process, all subjects were unfamiliar to the author. The only contact person was the data collector, in most cases a teacher, who also chose the sample. All collectors were provided with an electronic copy of the questionnaire, the answer sheet and all necessary instructions which were also printed on the answer sheet. The information was handed out almost simultaneously, but the return depended on the size of the sample. The predefined minimum was 30 students per group. Participants received a hardcopy of the questionnaire.[31] They had no aid and 10 minutes to

---

[30] The pretest data are in the file "Pretest", available upon request.
[31] The study was not available online as such unobserved calibration studies can hardly be valid.

answer all questions. There was no feedback available during the test. However, subjects received the correct answers after the collection of every paper.

Although the data collectors did not report an incidence, there were 10 unusable responses. The students stated no or obviously fake responses about age, gender, and level of education. These papers received a chronological number but were not used for data analysis. In addition, there were a few students who forgot to write down their age. The necessary information was provided by their teachers or estimated based on the average age of their classmates. Several participants did not answer all 10 questions. This is a typical behavior of pupils who do not think that they know the answer. They do not respond even if it is just an estimate. Russo and Schoemaker (1992) argue that a lack of knowledge is no excuse for an overly-narrow CI. This is also true for the missing answers. It is not a sign of a calibrated person but it does not prove overconfidence either. There is a special count for these cases in the code plan. Each of these questionnaires was analyzed to determine whether the missing interval can be seen as a correct, an incorrect or an invalid answer. In many cases the students stated their best estimate but no interval. The chance of being correct was assessed based on the given information. Generally, the comparison of the sample means of those with ($\bar{x} = 1.59$, n=489, SE=0.061) and without ($\bar{x} = 1.7$, n=46, SE=0.196) all intervals showed no proof of a statistically significant difference (p=0.61) in accuracy between the two groups. Therefore, there is no evidence that subjects with missing intervals would estimate any differently than their classmates. The accuracy was not calculated from the number of remaining questions and answers because this would lead to statistical artifacts. A student who only estimates questions he knows for sure would have an unrepresentatively high level of accuracy. All author's remarks on the questionnaires are in red. These are namely the code plan items to ease the data implementation.

5.3 Findings

Six schools and one university with a total of 545 students participated in the survey. 258 male and 277 female students gave valid responses. 10 subjects gave invalid answers which represents 1.8% of all participants. The youngest subject was 13, the oldest 27 years old. 79.3% were 18 or younger. The vast majority showed a distinct overconfident behavior in their decision making. 91.6% had three or less correct answers within their 90% CI. Two students were calibrated (A=9); both females from SSS and vocational school. Two male commercial school students had accuracy of 7. The average accuracy was 1.6 (N=535, σ=1.354). Undergraduates had the highest group average accuracy of 2.03 (n=30, SE=0.251) followed by SSS students with 1.87 (n= 52, SE=0.227). The NRW Realschule pupils showed the highest overconfidence level with an average of 8.1 which is equal to 0.9 correct answers out of 10 (n=61, SE=0.132). The Hauptschule ninth graders were slightly better with 0.94 (n=34, SE=0.174). An explorative analysis using Kolmogorov-Smirnov and Shapiro-Wilk tests shows that the data is not normally distributed with a significance < 1‰.[32] The Central Limit Theorem says that if *"X* [data] *is nonnormal, $\bar{X}$* [sample] *is approximately normal for sufficiently large sample sizes. The definition of 'sufficiently large' depends on the extent of nonnormality of X"* (Keller, 2005). Given the large sample size and the robustness of the analysis of variance (ANOVA) against nonnormality, the Levene's test provides the crucial information about homogeneity of variance. Homoscedasticity was implied as all test results were non-significant. Due to nonnormal distribution, the Mann-Whitney approach replaced the standard t-test for comparing two means.

The first step's hypothesis was tested with ANOVA and revealed a significant difference between Gymnasium ($\bar{x} = 1.7$, n=119, SE=0.106), Hauptschule, and commercial school students ($\bar{x} = 1.8$, n=82, SE=0.171). The one-way analysis shows that with F=5.765 the p-value=0.004 (<α=0.05) and the null hypothesis can be rejected. Observing the contrast coefficients, it becomes clear that the Hauptschule ninth graders differ from their Gymansium and commercial school counterparts. There is no statistical significance between the two last mentioned groups.[33] For the next hypothesis test the vocational students were divided in VA-Classes ($\bar{x} = 2.03$, n=35, SE=0.285) and VM-Classes ($\bar{x} = 1.55$, n=122, SE=0.109). They were compared to each other and to SSS students. The one-way ANOVA could not prove a significant difference between the three groups (F=2.004, p=0.137). The contrast test showed similar findings. Therefore, H_0 cannot be rejected. The last of the three

---

[32] The research question determines nonnormality. Ninth graders are overrepresented and the average number of correct answers is in the lower third.
[33] All results can be found on the data disc (available upon request) in the file "Results.spv".

steps compared students with the longest secondary education (Gymnasium) to those with the highest overall education (TUM). The Mann-Whitney U test stated that there is no statistically provable evidence that behavior under uncertainty varies between undergraduates and ninth graders. Z=-1.04 and p=0.298. The assumed equality of H_0 cannot be rejected.

5.4 Interpretation

The numbers paint a clear picture. There is significant discrepancy among accuracy of ninth graders. Hauptschule pupils had the lowest sample mean of correct answers within a 90% CI. They showed excessively overconfident behavior in the task but this is true for all groups. The average subject had 1.6 correct answers out of 10. The target accuracy was 9. These findings are congruent with previous studies in this field. Overconfidence is the norm, accuracy seldom, and underconfidence a phenomenon. The majority was younger than 18 and puberty could have biased the results. Therefore, subjects were grouped in 5-years intervals ranging from 13 to 17 ($\bar{x} = 1.50$, n=330, SE=0.074), from 18 to 22 ($\bar{x} = 1.79$, n=170, SE=0.104), and from 23 to 27 ($\bar{x} = 1.65$, n=35, SE=0.231). If biochemical processes influence participants' overconfidence level, there should be a positive correlation between age and accuracy. The results of a one-way ANOVA suggest otherwise. With F=2.632 and p=0.073, the hypothesis that all age groups show equal accuracy cannot be rejected. Moreover, the contrast test shows that the only significant difference is between 13 – 17 and 18 – 22 with T=-2.284 and p=0.023 (<α=0.05). A significant proof of a gap between the youngest and the oldest group was not given (T=-0.617, p=0.538). The analysis reveals that it is unlikely that age confounded the results of this study. Subitem 4.1.1 described men's tendency towards overconfidence. The fact that an almost equal amount of male ($\bar{x} = 1.73$, n=258, SE=0.084) and female ($\bar{x} = 1.48$, n=277, SE=0.081) students participated, provided an incentive to test whether gender could have influenced the results. With 95%, confidence the null hypothesis saying that there is no gender gap can be rejected (T=2.16, p=0.031). Although H_1 cannot be tested, female students were on average more overconfident than their male classmates.

The applicability is another important aspect to this research paper. The question is, if the findings would have been the same in another federal state. If there is no difference, NRW Realschule and Bavarian commercial school ninth graders will show similar accuracy levels as both groups receive the same school leaving certificate. The Mann-Whitney U test reveals the counter argument with p<1‰ (Z=-3.87). The approximate answer is No; they do not have the same level of overconfidence. The findings cannot be converted to other states and may only be applicable to the Bavarian education system. A nationwide research with all school types from every federal state is necessary to examine common behavior.

6 CONCLUSION

For centuries philosophers have stressed the importance of metaknowledge. Confucius once said *"To know that we know what we know and that we do not know what we do not know, that is true knowledge"* (Russo and Schoemaker, 1992). Only 2 students (0.4%) realized that the 10 questions are beyond their knowledge. They recognized the difficulty of the task and chose a wide CI. There was no hint, no advice, and no remark that subjects should not use an extremely wide or overly-narrow interval. 533 participants decided themselves to estimate the answer in a small range of subjective probability. They failed to acknowledge that these questions are not answerable applying the methodology of a "realistic" guess; especially not within a 90% CI. It may seem surreal that Greenland's coast is more than 4,000 kilometers longer than the circumference of the earth at the equator or that Hong Kong consists of 264 mostly uninhabited islands. In that aspect a correct estimate is unrealistic, a logical CI is not. To answer the research question, if overconfidence is a matter of education: Yes, to a certain extent it is. The Kruskal-Wallis test substantiating the finding that the hypothesis saying there is no difference among the various school types can be rejected (p<1‰). Hauptschule and NRW Realschule ninth graders showed the highest overconfidence level and can be put in a homogeneous subgroup. Once education reached a certain level, it does not significantly increase accuracy any more. On average, undergraduates of one of Germany's most prestigious universities did not do any better than vocational students holing a tertiary entrance certificate. Furthermore, there was no significant proof that university students chose their 90% CI any better than Gymnasium ninth graders. Age does not positively correlate with accuracy. In fact, the oldest participant, a 27-year-old TUM undergraduate, had one correct answer and the youngest, a Gymnasium student aged 13, had three correct answers. The gender gap did not occur in its usual way and Bavarian commercial school students did better on the test than their NRW counterparts. All these findings leave the basic problem untouched. 99.6% of all subjects did not sufficiently recognize the level of difficulty. More education only works to a certain extent and an increase in age does not help either. The heuristic is part of human nature but, as mentioned above, it can have a severe impact. In some cases it may cause loss of money or lead to divorce but in a few cases, the misjudgment could end in a catastrophe taking thousands of lives. Scholars found ways to improve calibration and to prevent the harmful effects of the distortion of judgment. Awareness should doubtlessly be the first step. Schools can improve their students' metaknowledge by creating awareness for the issue and its causes. They can introduce case studies dealing with situations of misjudgment and its effects (Russo and Schoemaker, 1992). These sessions should result in clear and direct feedback to guarantee sustainable development. Although this study involves various educational institutions and a sufficient amount of subjects, it cannot reflect society as a whole. There are different private institutions such as Montessori and Waldorf schools or residential schools which apply different teaching styles and educational methodologies. They represent a certain share of the population of students and should be included in further research. A nationwide study including all 16 federal states with their different schools and universities may be part of future analysis. As a consequence of the findings, the development and effectiveness testing of case studies aiming for improvement of metaknowledge in schools can certainly be another interesting task. In the future, there will be many other papers analyzing overconfidence. They will provide new insights and determinants. The studies will help us to understand unknown aspects of the heuristic but, hopefully, they will also recommend preventive measures against its harmful aspects. At the moment, we still have to gather information but sooner or later the causes have to be neutralized. On Super Tuesday, February 5, 2008, Barack Obama gave a speech about change. He said "*We are the ones, we've been waiting for*". It is questionable if the current generation has learned to listen to ancient philosophers who demanded wiser decision making. There are two possibilities: we accept the limits of our own influence and knowledge, or we keep on waiting because, for now, we are not the ones we've been waiting for.

V BIBLIOGRAPHY

Baker, L.A., Emery, R.E., 1993. When Every Relationship is Above Average: Perceptions and Expectations of Divorce at the Time of Marriage. Plenum Publishing Corporation.

Bank, M., Kottke, N., 2005. Die Auswirkungen von Overconfidence auf die Rationalität von Entscheidungen.

Barber, B.M., Odean, T., 2001. Boys will be boys: Gender, overconfidence, and common stock investment. Quarterly Journal of Economics 261–292.

Bavarian State Government, 2003. The Future Lies in Education [WWW Document]. Free State of Bavaria. URL http://www.bayern.de/The-Future-Lies-in-Education-.607/index.htm [Date of Query: July 4, 2012]

Benoit, J.P., Dubra, J., 2009. Overconfidence?

Brenner, L.A., Koehler, D.J., Liberman, V., Tversky, A., 2004. Overconfidence in probability and frequency judgments: A critical examination. Organizational Behavior and Human Decision Processes 65, 212–219.

Bryan, N., 2003. Bhopal: Chemical Plant Accident. Gareth Stevens Pub.

Burger, J.M., Schnerring, D.A., 1982. The Effects of Desire for Control and Extrinsic Rewards on the Illusion of Control and Gambling. Motivation and Emotion 6, 329 – 335.

Camerer, C., Lovallo, D., 1999. Overconfidence and excess entry: An experimental approach. The American Economic Review 89, 306–318.

Campbell, C., Van der Wende, M., 2000. International initiatives and trends in quality assurance for European higher education. ENQA occasional paper 1.

Campbell, W.K., Sedikides, C., 1999. Self-Threat Magnifies the Self-Serving Bias: A Meta-Analytic Integration. Review of General Psychology 3, 23 – 43.

Cooper, A.C., Woo, C.Y., Dunkelberg, W.C., 1988. Entrepreneurs' Perceived Chances for Success. Institute for Research in the Behavioral, Economic, and Management Sciences, Krannert Graduate School of Management, Purdue University.

Crawford, J.D., Stankov, L., 1996. Age differences in the realism of confidence judgements: A calibration study using tests of fluid and crystallized intelligence. Learning and Individual Differences 8, 83–103.

Daniel, K.D., Hirshleifer, D., Subrahmanyam, A., 2001. Overconfidence, arbitrage, and equilibrium asset pricing. The Journal of Finance 56, 921–965.

Diamond, P.A., Vartiainen, H., 2007. Behavioral Economics and Its Applications. Princeton University Press.

El-Gamal, M.A., Grether, D.M., 1995. Are People Bayesian? Uncovering Behavioral Strategies. Journal of the American Statistical Association 90, 1137 – 1145.

European Commission, 2011. The Bologna Process - Towards the European Higher Education Area [WWW Document]. Education & Training. URL http://ec.europa.eu/education/higher-education/doc1290_en.htm [Date of Query: July 4, 2012]

European Commission, 2012. Erasmus - Facts, Figures & Trends.

Grömminger, T., 2011. Rationalitätsdefizite: Herausforderungen für das Controllingprofil am Beispiel der Budgetierung im Kontext des verhaltensorientierten Controllings. GRIN Verlag.

Guenther, C.L., 2009. Deconstructing the better-than-average effect.

Hackl, T., 2004. Wiederholen da Vorrücken nicht erlaubt [WWW Document]. Staatliche Schulberatung in Bayern. URL http://www.schulberatung.bayern.de/schulberatung/bayern/schullaufbahnberatung/schullaufbahnen/gymnasium/index_05735.asp [Date of Query: July 4, 2012]

Hall, C.C., Ariss, L., Todorov, A., 2007. The illusion of knowledge: When more information reduces accuracy and increases confidence. Organizational Behavior and Human Decision Processes 103, 277–290.

Harvey, J.H., Ickes, W.J., Kidd, R.F., 1978. New Directions in Attribution Research. Routledge.

Hershey, D.A., Wilson, J.A., 1997. Age differences in performance awareness on a complex financial decision-making task. Experimental Aging Research 23, 257–273.

IAEA, 2010. INES [WWW Document]. International Atomic Energy Agency. URL http://www.iaea.org/Publications/Factsheets/English/ines.pdf [Date of Query: July 4, 2012]

IAEA Expert Mission, 2011. Preliminary Summary of the Nuclear Accident following the Great East Japan Earthquake and Tsunami [WWW Document]. Nuclear and Industrial Safety Agency. URL http://www.nisa.meti.go.jp/english/files/en20110601-1.pdf [Date of Query: July 4, 2012]

Iyengar, S.S., Lepper, M.R., 2000. When choice is demotivating: Can one desire too much of a good thing? Journal of personality and social psychology 79, 995.

Kahneman, D., Slovic, P., Tversky, A., 1982. Judgment under Uncertainty: Heuristics and Biases, First Edition, Later Printing. ed. Cambridge University Press.

Keller, G., 2005. Statistics for Management and Economics, 7th ed. ed. Cengage Learning Services.

Kovalchik, S., Camerer, C.F., Grether, D.M., Plott, C.R., Allman, J.M., 2005. Aging and decision making: A comparison between neurologically healthy elderly and young individuals. Journal of Economic Behavior & Organization 58, 79–94.

Krugman, P., 2007. Who Was Milton Friedman? The New York Review of Books.

Kyodo News, 2012. Nuclear agency, TEPCO knew in 2006 tsunami could trigger power loss. Kyodo News Network.

Lecture 4: Conditional Probability, Total Probability, Bayes's Rule, 2005. .

Li, S., Chen, W.W., Yu, Y., 2006. The reason for Asian overconfidence. The Journal of Psychology 140, 615–618.

Lundeberg, M.A., Fox, P.W., Punṯcoha•, J., 1994. Highly confident but wrong: Gender differences and similarities in confidence judgments. Journal of Educational Psychology 86, 114–121.

Masaya, Y., 2012. Causes and Countermeasures: The Accident at TEPCO's Fukushima Nuclear Power Station [WWW Document]. Nuclear and Industrial Safety Agency. URL http://www.nisa.meti.go.jp/english/files/en20120321.pdf [Date of Query: July 4, 2012]

Mayrhofer, W., 2006. Overconfidence and Rank. Kufstein.

Müller, A., 2007. Impact of Overoptimism and Overconfidence on Economic Behavior: Literature Review, Measurement Methods and Empirical Evidence. GRIN Verlag.

Nobel, C., 2011. Why Companies Fail--and How Their Founders Can Bounce Back [WWW Document]. HBS Working Knowledge. URL http://hbswk.hbs.edu/item/6591.html [Date of Query: July 4, 2012]

Nobel Lectures, 1967. Physics 1901 - 1921. Elsevier Publishing Company, Amsterdam.

OECD, 2012. What PISA Is [WWW Document]. PISA. URL http://www.pisa.oecd.org/pages/0,3417,en_32252351_32235907_1_1_1_1_1,00.html [Date of Query: July 4, 2012]

Oskamp, S., 1965. Overconfidence in case-study judgments. Journal of consulting psychology 29, 261.

Oxford Advanced Learner's Dictionary of Current English, 7. Auflage. ed, 2005. . Oxford University Press.

Russo, J.E., Schoemaker, P.J.H., 1992. Managing Overconfidence. Sloan Management Review 33, 7 – 17.

Schwartz, B., 2005. The Paradox Of Choice: Why More Is Less. HarperCollins.

ShanghaiRanking Consultancy, 2011. Academic Ranking of World Universities [WWW Document]. ARWU. URL http://www.shanghairanking.com/ARWU2011.html [Date of Query: July 4, 2012]

Shead, N.W., Hodgins, D.C., Scharf, D., 2008. Differences between Poker Players and Non-Poker-Playing Gamblers. International Gambling Studies 8, 167–178.

Shefrin, H., 2002. Beyond Greed and Fear: Understanding Behavioral Finance and the Psychology of Investing, Revised ed. Oxford University Press.

Sherrill, M., 2007. Self-Serving Bias. International Encyclopedia of the Social Sciences 2, 429.

Shiller, R.J., 2000. Irrational Exuberance, illustrated ed. Princeton University Press.

Spring, J.H., 2000. The Universal Right to Education: Justification, Definition, and Guidelines. Taylor & Francis.

Steinberg, R.M., 2011. Governance, Risk Management, and Compliance: It Can't Happen to Us--Avoiding Corporate Disaster While Driving Success. John Wiley and Sons.

Sunaoshi, H., Okuyama, T., Uechi, K., 2012. NISA kept U.S. plans for nuke plant failure to itself - AJW by The Asahi Shimbun [WWW Document]. AJW by The Asahi Shimbun. URL http://ajw.asahi.com/article/0311disaster/life_and_death/AJ201201270058 [Date of Query: July 4, 2012]

The Gallup Organization, 2009. Flash Eurobarometer 260 [WWW Document]. Students and Higher Education Reform. URL http://ec.europa.eu/education/higher-education/doc/studies/barometersum_en.pdf [Date of Query: July 4, 2012]

Tietze, J., 2011. Einführung in die Finanzmathematik: Klassische Verfahren und neuere Entwicklungen: Effektivzins- und Renditeberechnung, Investitionsrechnung, Derivative Finanzinstrumente, 11, akt. Aufl. 2011. ed. Vieweg+Teubner Verlag.

U.S. Census Bureau, 2012. Births, Deaths, Marriages and Divorces [WWW Document]. Statistical Abstract of the United States. URL http://www.census.gov/compendia/statab/2012/tables/12s0133.pdf [Date of Query: July 4, 2012]

UNESCO, 1997. International Standard Classification of Education 1997 [WWW Document]. URL http://www.unesco.org/education/information/nfsunesco/doc/isced_1997.htm [Date of Query: July 4, 2012]

UNESCO World Heritage Centre, 2011. The Great Wall - UNESCO World Heritage Centre [WWW Document]. URL http://whc.unesco.org/en/list/438 [Date of Query: July 4, 2012]

USGS, 2012. Earthquake Hazards Program [WWW Document]. U.S. Geological Survey. URL http://earthquake.usgs.gov/earthquakes/eqarchives/year/byyear.php [Date of Query: July 4, 2012]

Wiklund, J., 2006. Entrepreneurship: Frameworks and Empirical Investigations from Forthcoming Leaders of European Research. Emerald Group Publishing.

Yates, J.F., Lee, J.-W., Shinotsuka, H., 1996. Beliefs about Overconfidence, Including Its Cross-National Variation. Organizational Behavior and Human Decision Processes 65, 138–147.

VI APPENDIX

HOW WELL DO I ESTIMATE?

Things you do not know can be estimated. The following 10 questions are **estimation questions**. You start out by writing your most accurately estimated answer in the "blue" column. There is an <u>area</u> where the answer lies in your opinion, with **90% certainty**. Please fill your lowest estimate in the "green" column and your highest estimate in the "purple" column.

Here is an example: *Mrs. M. should estimate how often she will go to the cinema next year. She assumes 6- times, but is 90% sure that she will go to the cinema at least 4-times and the most 8-times. Her estimate looks as follows: at least 4, but the most 8 cinema visits.*

All questions should be answered on your own and without any tools and technical support!

	estimate	at least	the most
Example: How often will Mrs. M. go to the cinema next year?	6 times	4 times	8 times
1. How many kilometers air-line distance lie between Vienna and Rome?	km	km	km
2. Number of nuclear power plants in North America? (March 2012)	nuclear-power plants	nuclear-power plants	nuclear-power plants
3. How many female Nobel Prize winners are there?	Nobel-Prize winners	Nobel-Prize winners	Nobel-Prize winners
4. Number of civil airports (passenger airports) in the U.S. A.? (2011)	airports	airports	airports
5. Out of how many islands does Hong Kong exist?	islands	islands	islands
6. How long is the coast of Greenland?	km	km	km
7. How high is the second highest mountain of the Sothern Alps?	meters	meters	meters
8. How many shares has Google spent up to now? (31.03.2012)	shares	shares	shares
9. Number of native tree species in Germany?	tree species	tree species	tree species
10. How many inhabitants did the city London have in 1811?	inhabitants	inhabitants	inhabitants

For our statistics, we need a few more details: please tick the appropriate gender

    O male   O female   and your age: _____ years.

So far, what is your <u>highest reached level of education?</u> *Please tick one of the boxes*

So far no school leaving certificate	QLSGEC	GCSE	GCUASE	GCUE	Bachelor Degree
O	O	O	O	O	O

What is the **current** target level of education? *Please tick one of the boxes*

No aspired school leaving certificate	QLSGEC	GCSE	GCUASE	GCUE	Bachelor Degree
O	O	O	O	O	O

That was it. Thank you for your help!

A

WIE GUT KANN ICH SCHÄTZEN?

Dinge, die man nicht weiß, kann man auch schätzen. Die folgenden 10 Fragen sind **Schätzfragen**. Als erstes soll in der „blauen" Spalte die möglichst genau geschätzte Antwort eingegeben werden. Dann geht es um einen <u>Bereich</u>, in dem die Antwort Ihrer Meinung nach mit **90%iger Sicherheit** liegt. Die untere Schätzgrenze des Bereichs bitte in die „grüne" Spalte eintragen, die obere Schätzgrenze in die „lila".

Hier ein **Beispiel**: *Frau M. soll schätzen, wie oft sie nächstes Jahr ins Kino gehen wird. Sie vermutet 6-mal, aber sie ist sich zu 90% sicher, dass sie mindestens 4, aber maximal 8-mal ins Kino gehen wird. Ihre Schätzung sieht dann wie folgt aus: mindestens 4, aber maximal 8 Kinobesuche.* Alle Fragen sollen selbstständig und ohne Hilfsmittel beantwortet werden!

		Schätzung	Mindestens	Höchstens
Beispiel: Wie oft wird Frau M. nächstes Jahr ins Kino gehen?		6 mal	4 mal	8 mal
1.	Wie viele Kilometer Luftlinie liegen zwischen Wien und Rom?	km	km	km
2.	Anzahl an Atomkraftwerken in Nordamerika? (Stand März 2012)	Atomkraftwerke	Atomkraftwerke	Atomkraftwerke
3.	Wie viele Nobelpreisträger<u>innen</u> gibt es?	Preisträgerinnen	Preisträgerinnen	Preisträgerinnen
4.	Anzahl der zivilen Flughäfen (Passagierflughäfen) in den USA? (Stand 2011)	Flughäfen	Flughäfen	Flughäfen
5.	Aus wie vielen Inseln besteht Hong Kong?	Inseln	Inseln	Inseln
6.	Wie lange ist die Küste Grönlands?	km	km	km
7.	Wie hoch ist der zweithöchste Berg der Südlichen Alpen?	Meter	Meter	Meter
8.	Wie viele Aktien hat Google bisher ausgegeben? (Stand 31.03.2012)	Aktien	Aktien	Aktien
9.	Anzahl an einheimischen Baumarten in Deutschland?	Baumarten	Baumarten	Baumarten
10.	Wie viele Einwohner hatte die Stadt London im Jahre 1811?	Einwohner	Einwohner	Einwohner

Für unsere Statistik benötigen wir noch ein paar weitere Angaben: Bitte das zutreffende Geschlecht ankreuzen O männlich   O weiblich   und das Alter eintragen: _____ Jahre.

Was ist der <u>höchste, bisher erreichte</u> Bildungsabschluss? *Bitte nur ein Feld ankreuzen*

Bisher noch keinen Abschluss	Qualifiz. HS-Abschluss	Mittlere Reife	FH-Reife	Abitur/Matura	Bachelor-Abschluss
o	o	o	o	o	o

Was ist der **aktuell** angestrebte Bildungsabschluss? *Bitte nur ein Feld ankreuzen*

Keinen Abschluss angestrebt	Qualifiz. HS-Abschluss	Mittlere Reife	FH-Reife	Abitur/Matura	Bachelor-Abschluss
o	o	o	o	o	o

Das war´s auch schon. Vielen Dank für die Mithilfe!

B

ESTIMATION QUESTIONS - ANSWERS

First the answers of the following 10 questions should be **estimated**. After that an approximation within an interval is made in which the correct answer should lay between the lowest and highest estimate **in 9 out of 10 cases**.

Example: Mrs. M should guess how often she will go to the cinema next year. She thinks that she will go 6-times, but knows with a 90% confidence coefficient that she will at least go 4-times and at most 8-times. Her interval (here: 90% confidence coefficient =CI) is then as follows: [4-8]

All questions should be answered **independently** and **without involving any tools!**

Boundary conditions:

- no technical tools and support
- independent estimation without any other influence
- normally no longer than 10 minutes processing time
- All gaps and columns must be filled out

Example: How often will Mrs. M. go to the cinema next year?	Estimate: 6
	90%-CI: [4 – 8]
1. How many kilometers air-line distance lie between Vienna and Rome?	Answer: 766,289 km
2. Number of nuclear power plants in North America? (March 2012)	Answer: 124
3. How many female Nobel Prize winners are there?	Answer: 40
4. Number of civil airports (passenger airports) in the U.S. A.? (2011)	Answer: 5,175
5. Out of how many islands does Hong Kong exist?	Answer: 264
6. How long is the coast of Greenland?	Answer: 44,087 km
7. How high is the second highest mountain of the Sothern Alps?	Answer: 3,498 m
8. How many shares has Google spent up to now? (31.03.2012)	Answer: 326,010,000
9. Number of native tree species in Germany?	Answer: 72
10. How many inhabitants did the city London have in 1811?	Answer: 1,139,355

Sources:
1. http://www.luftlinie.org/Wien_Rom
2. http://www.euronuclear.org/info/encyclopedia/n/nuclear-power-plant-world-wide.htm
3. http://www.nobelprize.org/nobel_prizes/lists/women.html
4. http://www.bts.gov/publications/national_transportation_statistics/2011/html/table_01_03.html
5. http://www.auswaertiges-amt.de/DE/Aussenpolitik/Laender/Laenderinfos/01-Nodes_Uebersichtsseiten/Hongkong_node.html
6. https://www.cia.gov/library/publications/the-world-factbook/geos/gl.html
7. http://www.peakware.com/peaks.html?pk=247
8. http://finance.yahoo.com/q/ks?s=GOOG
9. http://www.zinkenundzapfen.de/uploads/media/Einheimische_Baumarten.pdf
10. http://www.demographia.com/dm-lon31.htm

SCHÄTZFRAGEN - ANTWORTEN

Die Antworten der folgenden 10 Fragen sollen zunächst geschätzt werden. Im Anschluss erfolgt eine Annäherung der korrekten Antwort innerhalb eines Intervalls, bei dem die korrekte Zahl **in 9 von 10 Fällen** zwischen der niedrigen und der hohen Schätzung liegen sollte. *Bsp.: Frau M. soll schätzen, wie oft sie nächstes Jahr ins Kino gehen wird. Sie vermutet 6-mal, aber sie ist sich zu 90% sicher, dass sie mindestens 4, aber maximal 8-mal ins Kino gehen wird. Ihr Intervall* (hier: 90%-Konfidenzintervall = **KI**) *sieht dann wie folgt aus: [4 – 8]*

Alle Fragen sollen **selbstständig** und **ohne Miteinbeziehung jedweder Hilfsmittel** beantwortet werden!

Randbedingungen:

- Keine Hilfsmittel
- Selbstständige Schätzungen ohne Beeinflussung
- In der Regel nicht länger als 10 Minuten Bearbeitungszeit
- Vollständigkeit aller auszufüllenden Felder muss gewährleistet sein

Bsp.: Wie oft wird Frau M. nächstes Jahr ins Kino gehen?	Schätzung: 6
	90%-KI: [4 – 8]
1. Wie viele Kilometer Luftlinie liegen zwischen Wien und Rom?	Antwort: 766,289 km
2. Anzahl an Atomkraftwerken in Nordamerika? (Stand März 2012)	Antwort: 124
3. Wie viele Nobelpreisträger**innen** gibt es?	Antwort: 40
4. Anzahl der zivilen Flughäfen (Passagierflughäfen) in den USA? (Stand 2011)	Antwort: 5175
5. Aus wie vielen Inseln besteht Hong Kong?	Antwort: 264
6. Wie lange ist die Küste Grönlands?	Antwort: 44.087 km
7. Wie hoch ist der zweithöchste Berg der Südlichen Alpen?	Antwort: 3498 m
8. Wie viele Aktien hat Google bisher ausgegeben? (Stand 31.03.2012)	Antwort: 326.010.000
9. Anzahl an einheimischen Baumarten in Deutschland?	Antwort: 72
10. Wie viele Einwohner hatte die Stadt London im Jahre 1811?	Antwort: 1.139.355

Quellen:
1. http://www.luftlinie.org/Wien_Rom
2. http://www.euronuclear.org/info/encyclopedia/n/nuclear-power-plant-world-wide.htm
3. http://www.nobelprize.org/nobel_prizes/lists/women.html
4. http://www.bts.gov/publications/national_transportation_statistics/2011/html/table_01_03.html
5. http://www.auswaertiges-amt.de/DE/Aussenpolitik/Laender/Laenderinfos/01-Nodes_Uebersichtsseiten/Hongkong_node.html
6. https://www.cia.gov/library/publications/the-world-factbook/geos/gl.html
7. http://www.peakware.com/peaks.html?pk=247
8. http://finance.yahoo.com/q/ks?s=GOOG
9. http://www.zinkenundzapfen.de/uploads/media/Einheimische_Baumarten.pdf
10. http://www.demographia.com/dm-lon31.htm

PARTICIPATING SCHOOLS AND INSTITUTES

Name	Address	Number of Participants
FosBos Rosenheim	Westerndorfer Straße 45, 83024 Rosenheim	52
Gymnasium Bad Aibling	Westendstr. 6A, 83043 Bad Aibling	122
Lise Meitner Realschule	Berliner Ring 5, 40789 Monheim am Rhein	63
Schulzentrum Blaufelden	Schulstraße 30, 74572 Blaufelden	34
Städtische Berufsschule für Versicherungswesen	Lincolnstr. 62, 81549 München	161
Technical University Munich	Arcisstraße 21, 80333 München	30
Wirtschaftsschule Alpenland	Westendstr. 6C, 83043 Bad Aibling	83

Code Plan

No.	Item	Explanation	Location on Questionnaire
1	lfd_nr	Chronological number per subject beginning with 1	
2	accuracy	Number of correct answers	
3	no_interval	Number of missing intervals	
4	gender	1 = male, 2 = female	
5	age	In years	
6	current_degree	0= No leaving certificate, 1=QLSGEC, 2=GCSE, 3=GCUASE, 4=GCUE, 5=Bachelor Degree	
7	future_degree	0= No aspired certificate, 1=QLSGEC, 2=GCSE, 3=GCUASE, 4=GCUE, 5=Bachelor Degree	

F